Unbelievable Pictures and Facts About Rabbits

By: Olivia Greenwood

Introduction

Not everyone knows a lot about rabbits. Many people just know that they breed a lot. There is much more to rabbits than the fact that they have lots of babies. Today we will be educating you as you learn lots of wonderful information about rabbits and everything that they have to offer.

Do rabbits get bored at all?

Just like rabbits do get bored often. If you have a pet rabbit it is important to ensure that your rabbit has enough space to move around and play. You can also buy toys for your rabbit and give it many things to chew, such as boxes. Rabbits are also much less bored if they have another rabbit friend to play with.

Are rabbits a good pet for children?

Rabbits are never good pets for children. They don't like being picked up and unfortunately, children may hurt or mistreat them by mistake. They are very delicate animals and children do not know how to look after them correctly.

Do animal shelters take in many rabbits?

This may be very interesting for you to learn, but animal shelters around the world actually take in more rabbits than they do dogs and cats.

Is it expensive to have a rabbit as a pet?

It is generally not too expensive to have a rabbit as a pet, although if your rabbit gets sick or needs a check-up it can become very expensive. Rabbits can not see normal dog and cat vets, they need to go to special exotic vets.

Does each rabbit have a different personality?

Just like dogs, cats, and even humans, every single rabbit is completely different and each one has its own distinct personality.

What particular rabbit breed is the smallest in the entire world?

The smallest breed of rabbits in the world is known as Netherland Dwarfs, they are very small and when they are babies they are tiny.

Are rabbits good or bad at jumping?

Rabbits are excellent at jumping and they are able to jump extremely high. Many rabbits have won world records for how high they can jump. There are many rabbit jumping competitions which are held all over the world.

Are rabbits clean animals or not?

Rabbits are actually extremely clean animals. They groom and clean themselves all the time. If you have a pet rabbit, you should never ever put it in water. They hate being bathed and the water will scare them. They are able to keep themselves clean at all times.

What are the biggest breed of rabbits that exist?

There are many different breeds that are rabbits, but the biggest breed is called flemish-giants. These rabbits can get really big, even bigger than the size of some dogs and cats.

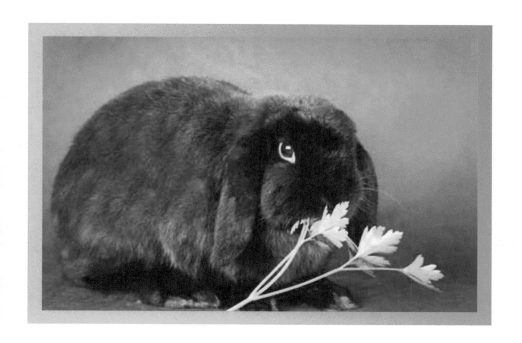

How do you know of a rabbit is happy?

You will actually be able to tell if a rabbit is happy. A rabbit binkies, where it runs up and down and jumps in the air. It is very cute and when a rabbit binkies this is a positive sign and it means that they are happy.

Are rabbits able to do tricks if taught?

There are many rabbits all over the world that can do tricks. Rabbits can get taught to do all sorts of wonderful and amazing tricks. Owners usually use food and their favorite treats to reward them.

Can you tame a rabbit?

Wild rabbits can be extremely wild. However rabbits can be tamed, if you tame a rabbit from birth and hand-rear the rabbits, they will grow up tame.

What is the average lifespan of a rabbit?

In the wild rabbits sometimes only live for around a year at a time, usually because they get eaten by other animals. However domesticated rabbits can live for around 7-10 years.

Do rabbits make good pets?

Rabbits make excellent pets, although you will really need to learn exactly how to look after them. Rabbits have very specific needs and they are very different from cats and dogs. They do make excellent pets and they are even able to bond with their owners. Some people allow their rabbits to sleep on their bed with them, the same way some people allow dogs and cats to sleep on a bed.

Are rabbits social animals or not?

Rabbits are extremely sociable animals. They always live together in groups. Even with pet rabbits, many people find it cruel to only have one rabbit. Rabbits enjoy bonding with other rabbits and they love to groom each other and look out for one another.

What is the name for baby rabbits?

The correct terminology which is used for a baby rabbit is a kit, this is short for kitten.

What do you call a female rabbit?

A female rabbit is usually called a doe.

What is the correct terminology for a male rabbit?

The correct terminology which is used for a male rabbit is a buck.

How many teeth does a rabbit have?

Although most people only know of rabbits front teeth, in total a rabbit has 28 teeth.

What types of food does a rabbit eat?

Rabbits eat all sorts of food when they are in the wild, things they typically eat are grass, fruits, and vegetables. Pet rabbits usually eat unlimited fresh hay , rabbit pellets and treat such as kale, spinach or even small pieces of carrot.

CPSIA information can be obtained
at www.ICGtesting.com
Printed in the USA
LVHW071138111119
636961LV00014B/3817/P